STUDY GUIDE

FOR NOVEL ONE

*Novel Edition

ISBN: 978-0-557-06516-5

Fiction

ISBN: **978-0-557-06516-5**

STUDY GUIDE

NOVEL ONE

*Novel Edition

By

Neebeeshaabookway

*For Use With The Jake Smith Ranch Series

~*~ TABLE OF CONTENTS ~*~

*http://go.neebeeshaabookway.com (free seizure info flyers)

INTRODUCTION TO BOOK'S PURPOSE:

INTRODUCTION TO BOOK'S PURPOSE:

Hey there and hello!

Author note:

The purpose of this FIRST section
is to give any of you pre-teens a preview of what to expect
and help you in your decision as to be reading this book—or—
on how you may share and use it for head injury awareness
and seizure awareness, along with,
tongue-loss awareness-issues.

*Some of you may even have family members, or friends that have lost part of their tongue, or their voice box, due to cancer—or have had a serious head injury from an accident—perhaps this book will help you understand the problems that they face, after you read these novels.

Thank you for your time, courtesy, and study, of this novel.
God bless, Neebeeshaabookway (Lizzy)

GOOD REASONS TO LEARN

GOOD REASONS TO LEARN:

More-and-more folks are finding themselves in the situation of having family members that have head injuries. The obstacles that folks, both with the injury, and those in the family, seek to deal with, are very strenuous, both mentally and physically.

This four-novel series about Jake and his twin Jade, seeks to show through an adventure in their lives—"fiction"—though based as close as possible, to facts, that:

1. Friends and family make a vast difference as one *heals*.
2. There is still a hope for joy and love to surround the home, through patience and learning "the trail".
3. And—that a fiction story can encourage folks to go out and learn more truth on these issues—and then, this book will have thankfully been *part* of some new *learning*, in your life, that led you to more learning tools.
4. And—hopefully it will be inspiration to you and your family, NOT to give up, while tackling your hard trail.

IN THIS FIRST NOVEL:

IN THIS FIRST NOVEL:

---

1. You will see how Jake comes home to a whole new world—though it is STILL his ranch-land home.

2. You will learn the how and why's as to his injury, and how his twin sister is the key to pulling him through this "new world" of "how to live".

3. You will see how good friends and buddies are needed—and you will see how many times, later on, the accident that injured your family member, MAY also have to be dealt with, by the one with the injury and by those in the close family circle as well. This helps with getting past it.

4. You get to see the victory that comes to Jake, one step at a time—it does not all come at once. It *grows*.

5. You learn a few insights as to how hard it is to live with seizures and tongue-loss—eating is very hard.

6. You get to see life move ahead, and out of the home, back into the open world of town, and of the public. A very needed, though hard step for anyone to make.

HOPEFULLY YOU ARE CURIOUS NOW:

HOPEFULLY YOU ARE CURIOUS NOW:

Here are a few things you can do now as you read the book, if you've chosen to buy any of the novels of the JAKE SMITH RANCH SERIES and it's short-stories of insight—or if it is just school work:

1. Find out what you can learn through the library, or, online, about head injuries (TBI).

2. Find out what you can learn through the library, or, online, about epilepsy (seizures).

3. Find out about tongue-loss. Many folks that suffer from this, have faced cancer, in the mouth, throat, or tongue-areas, and not as an injury such as Jake's. Yet, in rare incidences, folks have really lost their tongue (or part of it) in other ways.

- I -

WHO ELSE MAY LIKE THIS BOOK?

TWINS.

WHO ELSE MAY LIKE THIS BOOK?

TWINS.

This book is not only for those facing head injury issues, or any of the specific ones that Jake faces. This book has many benefits for those that are twins.

When a twin goes through a traumatic event, in a sense, the other twin travels this very same trail—through empathy. It is a very hard trail, twice as hard as other siblings in many hard-to-explain ways.

This is "your" twin book, with twin heroes, one that you will truly understand, whether you are fraternal, or identical.

- II -

WHO ELSE MAY LIKE THIS BOOK?

COWBOY RANCHERS.

WHO ELSE MAY LIKE THIS BOOK?

COWBOY RANCHERS.

YEP—Jake and his gang are ranchers from Montana. Well, seems they have moved up from Texas; though when quite *young*—but you get the drift. If you love working the great-outdoors, you have a deep feel for the book here, at hand.

Situations to conquer are not only in the home, but those due to *working situations* on the ranch. They also do trail-rides and trail-drives, so you will get the feel of what Jake has lost, and on what he hopes to gain back—if possible.

So—we now have a modern-day cowboy ranching story, as well.

- III -

WHO ELSE MAY LIKE THIS BOOK?

RODEO FOLKS.

WHO ELSE MAY LIKE THIS BOOK?

RODEO FOLKS.

Jake and his buddies, and even their families, have all come from the rodeo scene, and it taught them NOT to give up.

Hopefully there is enough feel from their life and enough mention of this, that you rodeo and ex-rodeo folks will "to home".

Their rodeo-riding is all done now, though, as Jake is their main focus in life now, and they chose to care for his needs.

Yet, for them, there is no regret—they are riding heroes for a good buddy now, and—their boss-man. This is their on-going work, and they all see the *new* goal.

- IV -

WHO ELSE MAY LIKE THIS BOOK?

FOLKS THAT KNOW OF GOD'S HELP.

WHO ELSE MAY LIKE THIS BOOK?

FOLKS THAT KNOW OF GOD'S HELP.

First-off, if you do not know how God can help you through your life—do not feel the book is not for you. God is moving in behind the scenes and YOU may not even know it!

The Jake Smith Ranch Series, does show examples of this, and how prayer helps when despair is pressing you beyond measure—and how relief can set in, after.

FOR those of you that DO know of how God moves through ones life, and how He is a great "restorer" you will take joy in seeing not only the story-line of God's way in this fiction book—but you will be triggered to remember all the ways that He has certainly been “behind the scenes” moving for you. God’s grace is all around us, if we will but take time to pray and thank Him. It all falls out of the hard “mines” of hardships and “pours out” into our grateful laps, then.

As you read this book, may you pray for help and grace for your injured family members—or for those that you know, or may not know, that are suffering from these very hard issues presented in this book.

And may God richly bless you
as you seek Him.

*And—thank you for taking a few moments to study-up on a bit of notes as to this book being a learning tool. Pass the word, around—love helps to overcome pain.

BEGIN:
STUDY-GUIDE QUESTIONS

(In Four Parts)

- USER GUIDE -

Use the page-title to start-off the questions, when the questions are NOT A FULL SENTENCE.

PART ONE - DO YOU REMEMBER DETAILS?

1. What time-frame did Jake arrive home from his very *first* hospital stay?

2. What are the “dancing angels”? What other things, *welcomed* Jake home?

3. What are the twins’ folks’ names? Where were the twins born?

4. What peculiar “action” did the twins learn from their pa? And—what word?

5. What two odd habits does Jade have, as to Jake? What does she call him?

6. What sign-system does Jade teach Jake? Who helps Jake learn to like it?

7. Who did Matt used to work for, and why did he quit? What did he learn?

8. Where did Stoney come from? Who were his folks? How did he get to Jake’s?

9. What were the bad deeds of Lyle? Why did he come to Montana?

10. How did Jade get Jake into town? What four things happened?

11. What are some of the dangers Jake faces, by having tongue-damage?

12. How did Lenny help Jake on his birthday? What is in Jake’s pocket?

13. Who are Vin and Carl, and what do they own? How did Jake know them?

14. What sadness is in Lolly’s family? How did Jake help her in the past?

15. What did the Baker’s give Jake in the hospital? What is the “myth”?

16. What kind of work do Jade and Galena do, in the basement?

17. Where is Honor from, and what kind of work does she do now?

18. What was Jake going to get from the kitchen, when he had the seizure?

19. Who were the ones hiding information from Jade, and why?

20. What does the ranch-gang do for relaxing, fun time, or evening time?

22. What are some of their holiday traditions of New Year, and Christmas?

23. What was Sofia’s previous home-life? Where are her folks?

24. Who had hired Sofia? Who had the job *before* her? What did Sofia learn?

25. What did Matt learn about Jake's watch? Why did this help Jake?

26. Who does Jake throw rocks at and why? But, at *home*, he does what?

27. What is the name of the river, and the creek? Why is the river important?

28. Who owns the Slipping Saddle? Who owns the Corner&Coffee? Drugstore?

29. How did Jake and Matt, first meet, later, what did they, *travel* to go do?

30. Why did Stoney ride the bull? Who else *could* have helped save him?

31. What was one of the main hard things Matt had to do, to save Jake's life?

32. How did Jade meet Lyle, and why did she decide to marry him?

33. What are the two main reasons that Jake did not like Miss Kaite around?

34. Why were there 3 birthday days, this year? What was done for each day?

35. Who felt to blame for Jake's accident? How did Stoney learn of Jake loss?

36. What two things prompted Jake to take seizure medication, finally?

37. Who is Hunter, and where did his mother live?

38. Who are the Cooks? Where do they live, and name them *all.*

39. What did Honor tell Jake he should do, and what did she give him?

40. Who thought Jake could really STILL talk? What happened after this?

41. What did Jake learn from cows, that helped him to communicate?

42. Who is the "flower"? Who is Spur-gal? Who is Harper?

43. What did Jake do, Jan. 2nd , one year after his accident?

44. What did Jake do, May 1st, one year after his homecoming?

45. What 3-4 conclusions did Jake come to decide?

46 – Make up your own question- write it in:

PART TWO - DO YOU REMEMBER KEY ISSUES?

1. **TALK ABOUT:** what Jake thought about in his room, before his sister came.

2. breakfast with Jade and why it was so hard on both of them.

3. why their first visitor was so unwelcomed, and who it was.

4. why the second visitor was more important, and how it helped.

5. why Jade had to follow her twin, what she did, and what happened after.

6. how Jake felt when he was with his horses, how it went from good to bad.

7. Jake's first phone call, and what his sister did, and why.

8. how and why the Bakers helped Jake on this first visit.

9. how Lolly helped Jake, and what she noticed.

10. the three people Jake met at the grocery store, and what he learned.

11. what Jake left at Lenny's and why—and why at first Jake felt lost.

12. talk about why Jade was upset with Jake, and what she learned.

13. why Ray brought the tape recording, and why such a last resort was used.

14, Jake's owl rescue, and the sorry results, for both Jake and Jade's plans.

15. talk about the sorrows of an old friend, named Mac, when he saw Jake.

16. how two deaf-folks using sign language made a world of life for Jake.

17. how Jake missed eating; how he ate now, and how others react.

18. how Jake met Sofia, and how he proceeded to court her, and who helps.

19. what happens during Jake's seizures, and what happens afterwards.

20. Jake and the dog rescue, and how it goes wrong.

22. how the police suspected Hunter's words, and why Hunter did this deed.

23. the dangers of having seizures, and how friends can help.

24. the hard burden of Stoney and Matt, keeping Jake's sudden secret.

25. how the wild turkeys were so important, as to timing.

26. why Jade broke-down after Lenny shared Lyle's past history.

27. how the river, and the woods always help Jake and/or Jade.

28. why Jade was never one to let romantic feelings turn to Stoney.

29. how and why Stoney waited for Jade, even though he secretly loved her.

30. how deep family commitments and love for their folks, helped the twins.

31. how and why, the boarding school had bad memories for the twins.

32. why Lyle wanted to marry Jade, and how he was going to hurt his folks.

33. why Jake didn't want to use a whistle, but *would* use pots and pans.

34. why Jake was drinking, and how it did harm in many ways.

35. how and why the twins are so close, and loyal to each other.

36. Jade, accepting Sofia, into their life, for Jake.

37. some ways that Jake felt at ease with Sofia

38. what all Jake was giving up, by not being out in his social circle and work.

39. how the river, in May, helped Jake realize something very serious.

40. Jake and Stoney, and how they both learned hard truth, in the woods.

41. why Christmas was so very sweet, and why Jade shared with Sofia.

42. how New Year's was hard at first, but became better, for two reasons.

43. how and why Jan 2nd was hard, but needed to be conquered.

44. about Jake using his voice, and how and what he chose to do, if he did.

45. how Honor's surprise visit, led Jake to stop being stubborn, to whistles.

46 – Make up your own question- write it in:

PART THREE - DO YOU REMEMBER NEW HOPE?

1. **WHAT KIND OF NEW HOPE CAME FROM ?** Ray's first morning arrival?

2. Jade hollering at her twin, on the ridge?.

3. Jake's first night on the sofa?

4. after Jake's arrest?

5. when Jade coaxed Jake to remember how they had childhood codes?

6. when Matt told Jade about Pedro, and Pedro, worked with Jake all day?

7. Jake going to town, to peek in on Sofia?

8. Jake's laryngitis escapade?

9. Jake and Ray's trick on Angie?

10. when Jake heard Pedro's voice and freedom?

11. when Sofia sat down at the Corner&Coffee, with Jake?

12. when Lenny went to learn more about Lyle?

13. when the police told Jake and Ray what Hunter had said?

14. when Matt, Galena, and Stoney, came back home to stay, again?

15. when the Bakers brought a bird-clock for the twins?

16. when the sign language books were left around the house?

17. when Jake finally learned he had a reading, writing, and number problem?

18. when Lenny put stickers on Jake's truck, and gave him a new "dog-tag"?

19. when Jake had the showdown with Angie?

20. when Lenny had told Jade about Lyle's evil deeds with the bull?

22. when Jake "fixed" his watch?

23. when Jake started using paper, finally?

24. when Jake started taking seizure medicine?

25. when Jade gave Jake a gift feeding tube (back during the hotel times)?

26. when Jade cut the feeding tube up, hanging it on the Christmas tree?

27. whenever the gang sat down to talk, in the evening on the porch?

28. when Matt went out to join Jake, on the year's anniversary of Jan 2nd?

29. during the accident, when Jade learned that Jake was not hunting?

30. during the accident, when Jake stepped into the round corral?

31. after Matt shares about the accident, and Jake finds some sap?

32. when Hunter arrives during the New Year?

33. when the gang does the "paper ripping", each year?

34. when Jake watches the Christmas lights dancing in the window?

35. when Jake signs to Jade, in the barn, on May 1st?

36. when Sofia sees that Jake lives near the Cook twins and their Pa?

37. when Jake was at his birthday party, listening to everyone talk?

38. when Jake ate cake at the Bakers?

39. when Jake first practiced the signs on his body, while fishing?

40. when Jake tried to speak to Jade, as a birthday present?

41. when Jade gave Jake a carved belt, as a birthday present?

42. when Jade rested her hand in Jake's armpit., when upset?

43. when a trail-ride come far-to-close to Jake, while he's fishing?

44. Honor's worries about Jade and Ray, after she shared with Jake?

45. when Honor visits Jake at the river, and he saves her?

46 – Make up your own question- write it in:

PART FOUR - WHAT WOULD YOU DO?

1. **OR-HOW WOULD YOU FEEL?** if you could not talk? If you could not eat?

2. about your friends always being on phones, but phones are useless to you?

3. would you miss singing? And being in the middle of conversations?

4. if someone in your family, suddenly had seizures? Or, if you did?

5. if someone you *knew* had a bad injury—would *you* know how to help them?

6. would you be able to be an anchor, or would you be too sad all the time?

7. if you had trouble trying to communicate, would you give up, or not?

8. you may not have a twin, but how do you treat your brother/sister, daily?

9. do you have loyal friends that help each other become strong and whole?

10. how do you suppose friendships are really made, and how to they last?

11. if you could not ever drive a car, or truck etc, again?

12. would you want other folks to watch you eat, if you ate in a odd manner?

13. if you finally met a gal/guy that you liked, and you could not talk to them?

14. if you spent a whole day NOT talking, like Jade tried to do, to understand?

15. if you were told you had a seizure, and you saw that you *wet* your pants?

16. if you had a seizure, and later learned, that everyone was staring at you?

17. if you had to use a special spoon and cup, to even swallow your food?

18. if you couldn't use letters, or talk, who would give you a job?

19. would you still get to go swimming and snow-boarding, or play hockey?

20. if you needed to mark time episodes, cause no one would help you?

22. if you had bad head aches all the time?

23. if you had damage in your leg or arm, and could not play or run?

24. if you couldn't talk, would you like to spend time in town, or at home?

25. would you like to go the grocery store, and malls, *alone*?

26. what are some good plans you could try to use, when you face the public?

27. if you met folks that can't talk—are you rude to them, do you ignore them?

28. if *you* saw someone have a seizure—*laugh* from the strangeness, or *not*?

29. would you laugh at your mother, sister, brother or father, if *they* had one?

30. if your folks, or grandparents had cancer and lost part of their tongue?

31. could or would you be patient, when they tried to talk to you?

32. would you finally ignore them, because it is too much work to understand?

33. if someone was *confused* from a head injury, and kept *repeating* things?

34. would you laugh; *call them retarded*? Do you <u>know</u> what <u>retarded</u> means?

35. if you heard some call someone retarded? Would you teach them truth?

36. would you be able to say, <u>people aren't retarded</u>, but their <u>brain</u> *can* be?

37. Jake's brain had retarded areas; can <u>you</u> honor such folks, as his friends did honor, him? Would you not want to because your friends would laugh at you? Brains are <u>fragile</u>, yours can "*break*" just as well as anyone else's.

38. would you take as long as Jake did, to go to town, or could you be braver?

39. if you were severely injured, would you work hard to get well, like Jake?

40. if you saved your friend's life—would you later be mad, if you were *hurt*?

41. could you be kind to someone like Hunter, after he said he was sorry?

42. if someone like Angie made fun of you—would you forgive her? or fight?

43. if your folks taught you about God and the Good Book? Would you care?

44. could you start your whole life over again, with it being <u>twice</u> as hard now?

45. could share these lessons with folks, to help them understand others?

<u>46 – Make up your own question- write it in:</u>

SCRIPTURE HELP THAT APPLIES, IF WANTED.

Romans 10:13
For whosoever shall call upon the name of the Lord shall be saved.

Timothy 4:18
And the Lord shall deliver me from every evil work,
and will preserve me unto his heavenly kingdom:
to whom be glory for ever and ever. Amen.

Philippians 4:13
I can do all things through Christ that strengthens me.

Romans 10:11
For the scripture saith, Whosoever believeth on him shall not be ashamed.

Acts 19:2
He said unto them, Have you received the Holy Ghost since you believed?
And they said unto him, We have not so much as heard
whether there be any Holy Ghost.

James 5:16b
The effectual fervent prayer of a righteous man availeth much.

May God bless you – **Thank you so very much for reading THE JAKE SMITH RANCH SERIES!**

FROM: THE HOLY BIBLE

The King James Version
The World Publishing Company

ISBN: 978-0-557-06516-5

FICTION:

www.ingramcontent.com/pod-product-compliance
Ingram Content Group UK Ltd.
Pitfield, Milton Keynes, MK11 3LW, UK
UKHW041836200726
13854UKWH00003BA/1172